Stirr It Up

A yabba pot bubbling with performance poetry, storytelling and traditional practices in
Montserrat – The Emerald Isle of the Caribbean

Poems and Short Stories

By

Maureen "Greer" Lee

"The Sankofa Lady"

Copyright

Copyright @2025 by Maureen "Greer" Lee
Cover photography @ 2025 by Isaiah Harrigan
Photo edit @ 2025 by Marvin Meade
Internal design @2025 by Alicia 'Molly' Barzey
Short Stories edit @2025 by Cereen Harrigan

All rights reserved. No part of this book may be reproduced in any form or by any electronic or mechanical means, including information storage and retrieval systems, except in the case of brief quotations embodied in critical articles or reviews, without permission in writing from its author.

ISBN 979-8-89571-193-4 (Paperback)

Dedication

This book is dedicated to my ancestors who walked before me and paved the way for my Sankofa journey. It is also dedicated to the fruits of my womb – Myron and Cereen and their children – Isaiah, Lea and Zachary. You make my heart smile.

Acknowledgment

I would like to thank the Most High for the gift of life, knowledge, a wise mind and inner standing.

Writing a book is a totally different ball game to performing on stage. None of this would have been possible without my cousin, my sister, my confidant, my beloved – Alicia "Molly" Barzey. You have been the wind beneath my wings throughout the years, propelling me to soar. Your commitment, dedication, professionalism and expertise helped to bring this book to fruition.

My daughter Cereen and grandson Isaiah for your love, support and technical assistance.

Marvin Meade (Photographer) for your incredible work on the cover photo which brought my vision for this book to life.

Melvin "Takumah" Galloway for your unwavering support.

… and anyone who contributed in any way along this journey to help make this book become a reality, I am eternally grateful.

Table of Contents

Copyright ii
Dedication iii
Acknowledgment iv
Preface... viii
Definition ix
Yabba Pot x
Sankofa.. xi
Gye Nyame.. xii
SECTION 1 13
Virtuous Woman 15
Rise Woman, Rise... 17
Phenomenal Women of Montserrat 19
I Am She – African Royalty.....................................23
Don't Cry, Mama 25
My Mama 28
Happy Mother's Day..30
Sistah Empress 32
Wombman – The Life Force 35
Empress Roll Call 36
Access Denied..38
Caribbean Woman...41
Come ReasonWith Me 42
Queen Mother Roberts 46

v

Lady of Grace 47

Birth of an Angel 48

Get Ready and Stay Ready 50

Just A Rose Will Do 52

Beauty for Ashes 55

Smile for Life 56

Four Hundred Years and Counting 58

You Are an African Child 60

The Confession 62

Let it be God 64

Standing on the Promises of God 66

Practical Application 68

A Wa Dem A Teach Dem 70

By What Measure 72

Shattering Glass Ceilings 74

I Am Sorry That You Are Sorry 76

Blessed Father's Day 81

The Sax Man 83

Montserrat Strong 84

Back to Montserrat Sistah Flarry 86

Taste Of The Caribbean 88

SECTION 2 92

How Sissy Donkey Lost Her Tail 94

Hold Him Joe 98

Give The Child My Name 100

Back To The Dust 102

Rum 'Till I Die..105

The Cesspool Rules..107

No Nose Leah...109

How The Fairy Healed My Crappax 111

Penny Fart 113

Nick Names..115

SECTION 3 117

Body, Mind & Spirit 118

Mother Earth Beckons...119

Natural Livity...120

Healing of the Nation 121

Nature's Medicine Chest..122

Glossary………………………………….……………....…123

Preface

STIRR It Up Is a Yabba pot bubbling with performance poetry, folk tales, and bush medicine by The Sankofa Lady. It is an ital, which is vital for the body, mind, and soul. She transports you on a Sankofa journey, riding on the backs of our elders and wings of our ancestors to a place where the supernatural was natural, where there was still unity in the community and where one can actually make sense out of nonsense. This collection of poems, short stories and cultural practices was passed down orally through generations within the Montserrat community. These poems and stories serve to edutain, explain natural phenomena and convey moral lessons. They reflect the beliefs, values and traditions of our people. So, grab a calabash and indulge in this cultural delicacy. It makes for an eclectic *tea/coffee table* book experience.

Definition

Yabba Pot

A **Yabba pot** is a traditional earthenware cooking pot used in Rastafarian culture. These pots, traditionally made from local clay and fired in a kiln, are used for slow cooking "ital" food, a cuisine focused on natural organic, and unprocessed foods. The Yabba pot symbolizes community connection and the importance of grounding oneself in nature.

Sankofa

SANKOFA, derived from the Akan language of Ghana, means "to go back and get it" "learn from the past to move forward". It emphasizes the importance of reflecting on history and experience to inform future actions and progress. The concept is often represented by a mythical bird with its head turned backward, carrying an egg in its mouth, symbolizing the past and the future.

Gye Nyame

The symbol of God's omnipotence

The I AM that I AM

From whom I seek ultimate guidance

The ALPHA and OMEGA

The beginning and the end

My Master, my Saviour, my Comforter, my Friend.

SECTION 1
DUB POETRY

Dub Poetry is a form of performance poetry rooted in African tradition that blends spoken words with rhythms and instrumentation.

Sankofa Lady Speaks

A woman who feareth the Lord, she shall be praised.......

Virtuous Woman

Who can find a virtuous woman ?
For her price is far above rubies
Many have done virtuously have heeded the call
but we are the authentic ones who excellest them all
From the sole of our feet to the crown on our head
our children arise and call us blessed
Strength and honor are our clothing
we shall rejoice in time to come
On our tongue is the law of kindness
we openeth our mouths with wisdom
Our candle goeth not out by night
for we walk by faith and not by sight
We are not idle with our hands
for a vineyard we plough the lands
Now, we all know that favor is deceitful
and beauty is vain
So, virtuous ones, let our anthem raise
a woman who feareth the Lord, she shall be praised.

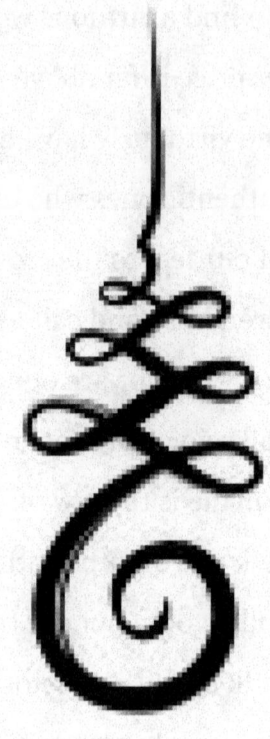

Rise Woman, Rise

Rise woman, rise

Arise and shine for thy light is come

and the glory of Jah is upon thee – rise

Rise up ye women who are at ease

tremble, be troubled

Now put on your khaki suits and Gideon boots

It's time to Jihad for righteousness and truth

Put on your garments of praise

for the spirit of heaviness

Woman of Judah, thou art lioness

So, rise woman, rise- rise woman, rise

Rise woman, rise

Arise and shine for thy light has come

and the glory of Jah is upon thee

Goddess, Empress, Daughter of Zion

Queen Omega – Mother of Creation

Rise.

Your courage and grace go hand in hand......

Phenomenal Women of Montserrat

Phenomenal women of Montserrat
Great grandmothers, grandmothers, mothers,
daughters, sisters, aunts, nieces, and others
I see you, I hear you, I feel you, I am you
I love your class, feel your passion and style
ye phenomenal women of the Emerald Isle
The way you move, the way you groove
you are oh, so dignified and eloquent
with such charisma, morals and natural talent
Immaculate in your standing
virtuous in your ways
comely, exquisite, captivating
long-suffering throughout your days
Exemplary, honorable, faithful
vibrant, dedicated, loyal to your land
Your courage and grace go hand in hand
Lava warrior queens, you are hot, hot, hot
Ye phenomenal women of Montserrat.

Despite the fact that you despise the fact.......

You Are A Strong Woman

Despite the fact that you despise the fact
you are expected to act and not re-act
For the role of an activist
is not played by a re- activist
Having a heart of gold
means that you can neither be bought nor sold
And although you may be treated like spit
you're not entitled to throw a fit
We live in a plastic world, my child
So, put on that plastic smile
You are a strong woman
But don't cry for me, just be willing to die for me
Or let's simply agree to disagree
For sooner or later, the tables will definitely turn
and it will no longer be theirs, but your turn
No longer will you be kissing brass
You will now be kicking past
those who decisively used and misused you
Declaring judgment, having no mercy
No longer able to feel
the agony of their crushed heads under your
Gideon boot heel
For they named it, and you claimed it
You are a strong woman.

I am she ...

*Empress Authentic, Sankofa Lady,
Lava Warrior Queen - African Royalty-*

I Am She – African Royalty

I am she, African royalty
Although I was not born in Africa
Africa was born in me
Empress Menen, Makeda, The Queen of Sheba
Neferteri, Nzingha, Nandi, Amina
I am diverse in tribe and ethnicity
Maasi, Yoruba, Zulu, Ashanti
Karo, Himba, San, Hadzabe
I am the fertile River Nile
always relevant, forever in style
South to north is my standard flow
covering eleven countries including the Congo
I am a Moor for sure, no less
Inventor of navigation techniques
Astronomy, I am the original architect
I am Rosa and hell yes, I made a fuss
No longer will we sit in the back of the bus

Like Angela Davis' serenity prayer intellect
no longer will we accept the things
we cannot change
We will change the things we cannot accept
I am Harriet – a woman called Moses
conveying from the grave
that I freed a thousand
and could have freed a thousand more
if only they knew that they were slaves
I am Massa's worse nightmare
the Warrior NuNu with the drop-dead stare
I am kick-butt Nanny
Winnie and the Fire Burn Queens
the mean machine Wangari Maathai
who planted trees and kept the belt green
I am Empress Authentic, Sankofa Lady
Lava Warrior Queen
I am she - African Royalty.

Don't Cry, Mama

When a gun son's Mama embraces him
she shouldn't cry when the judgment faces him
For it was just a matter of time
before he would pay for his life of crime
So don't cry, Mama
Dry the crocodile tears from your eyes, Mama
For when your child was being wicked and wild
you encouraged him in his life of crime
Bringing televisions and guns in and out of your house
while you're chilling like a couch potato
quiet like a church mouse
Now all of a sudden, you're calling the prayer line

In Father, Son, and Holy Ghost, you trust

when the church only sees you at Easter

funeral, wedding, New Year's, and Christmas

Pushing weed, coke and crack out of your yard

Just saying, "No !" what could have been so hard?

Oh, but the shopping sprees had your head turn

So, now let the law take its course

when judgment declares, "Burn Baby, burn."

But the good news is that God is not like man

He created us all with a master plan

So, should he repent and stop his dirty ways

Jah will forgive, bless, and lengthen his days

And tears of joy you shall then cry

as you give praises to the Most High

Now smile, Mama.

My Mama

R.I.P

My Mama

My mama was a strong, strong woman
She was 96 before she was caught at the boundary
She held her wicket, almost made a century
Like the one Jim Allen, she batted with style
She had Alzheimer's or some would call her senile
But she would tell you in a Montserrat minute
that she was far from being crazy
And to prove it, she would spell both of her names
Leah Greer and Catherine Lee
But do God bless you
don't ask her to tell you the two times table
her new and improved version
would make you laugh 'til you're not able
And towards the end you had to shout so loud
when talking to her
Lord knows it's true
not only our Father in heaven
but all the neighbors could hear you too

But don't let me get a telephone call
Her hearing would just return from a stroll in the park
And as blind as she claimed to be
she clearly saw my beautiful face
when she wants to sweet talk
If she didn't hear from you for a while
when you called, she would say
"tank Gad fu life, but eh, eh
wha happen, you dream dat me dead?"
What can you do but just laugh
and shake your head
Out of the blue, she sees a dog
running through the living room
and was always hungry, although you fed her
morning, night and noon
That's my Mama for you
humorous and with pearls of wisdom
I was honored not only to be her daughter
But her caregiver until His kingdom come.

Happy Mother's Day

So, it's your first Mother's Day in heaven
and I'm sure you had a ball
Somewhere around the throne of God
with your Pupa G, Ma, Aunt Sue, Uncle James,
Len, Ezra and the rest of them all
I must admit it was awkward for me down here

since this was your favorite day of the year

From the elaborate Montserratian breakfast

church service and lunch at Carambola

to visits from friends and relatives
who usually came from all over
You were really and truly missed this year
Even our grandeur plans could not compare
to seeing the broad smile on your face

and the twinkle in each eye
To be wrapped in your warm embrace
I must now look upwards to the sky
and say, "Blessed Mother's Day, Mama
Eternal be your rest
For you weren't just one in a million
You were the very best."

Sistah Empress

Sistah Empress Ijahnya

Woman of courage, roots and culture

Pan Africanist to the bone

Easy lay her crown

even when her pillow was made of stone

Like Mother Moses, she parted the Red Sea

exodused to Ethiopia to show you and me

life in Shashemane

Making a significant contribution from Anguilla

founding the Athyli Rogers Centre in Addis Ababa

Heartically ours, she will live on forever

our First Lady of Rasta – Sistah Empress Ijahnya.

Dedicated to the memory of Empress Ijahnya Christian- Afro-Anguillan social activist. (January 31, 1957 – April 27, 2020)

(Ras Bucket and Empress Authentic carrying the Empress Ijahnya banner in The Valley, Anguilla)

Ijahnya Christian was an Anguillan educator, writer and activist. She established the Tripple Crown Culture Yard in Anguilla. She moved to Shashemene, Ethiopia in 2010 to further her work in repatriating the African diaspora to the Mother Country. In that same year, she founded the Athlyi Rogers Study Centre, named after the Anguillan writer Robert Athlyi Rogers who wrote the Holy Piby (text of a religion called the Afro-Athlican Constructive Gaathly).

The channel through which all creation is birthed.....

Wombman – The Life Force

Whoever said that a woman is a delicate flower
petals to be plucked gently
moist like the mist of dew drops
in the early morning hour - was right
We are the measure of illuminous beauty
throughout the earth
The channel through which all creation is birthed
Once that water was released and the child came forth
we shifted gear to protector and defender
for all that it's worth
Our purpose is to give life, nurture life
to be influential as we guide life
to its highest developed realms of potential
There are times when we actually allow our higher
intelligence to guide the force and flow of our emotions
But at other times, the heat of response
provokes and controls our reactions
Be it on the frontlines or working behind the scenes
we have led troupes to many a victory using our
intuitive genes.

Empress Roll Call

Authentic Empresses do not try to impress
by flashing long locks and ankle length dress
smoking weed and modeling colors
but when you check their livity
they're not a blessing but a curse
Re-civilize yourselves, mothers of civilization
for in your bosom lies the gift of life
You are the Omega, you cradle creation
Return to thyself and take thy rightful place
dis-associate from all that is a disrespect
dishonor or disgrace
Learn the ways of the Queen Mother
Empress Menen First
Apply the Omega Principles in your daily trod
be at your best, not your worst
For she did not only talk the talk
building schools and orphanages
She walked the walk

I'm calling on my Sistren who fell out to fall in
Crown check, rule your queendom my queen
Let your actions speak loud
much louder than your words
Others will follow what they've seen
and not only what they've heard
For it's our burden to bear
crowns on our heads, cross on our shoulders
To feed them physically, mentally, spiritually
it's our God given nature to nurture
Love, honor, respect, humility
all signs of virtue
Adorn yourselves daily, call them forth
they're all in you
it's time for roll call
Call forth your Princess, Empress, Queen
Why sit ye idle woman
Empress Roll Call – Roll out or fall in.

Access Denied

Because I know myself, love myself, embrace my
Africanness and put my people first

means that I am strange, different and mad

Means that I am racist, prejudiced

everything but a child of God

I am not considered politically correct

for I rule my destiny, and the Babylon system reject

I refuse to be caught up in their colonial mess

staying true to my African heritage, royal bless

I am not deemed a success defined by cash

because I choose to sip less

from their bitter cup of hog wash

Seldom called upon to represent my nation

simply because I refuse to work

on their air-conditioned plantation

I've actually become

a second-class citizen in my own land

Overlooked, under-estimated, out-numbered

Someone please help me to understand

Is it my bongo natty, the locks on my head

or is it the nyabinghi judgement that they dread

For Jah knows, as much as I've been tested

And as much as I've tried

instead of a stamp of approval

all I keep on getting is Access Denied.

Caribbean women – we are the real deal……

Caribbean Woman

Caribbean women - we never claimed to be easy
despite the fact that our weather report is always fair to
partly cloudy with a chance of scattered showers
we are hot, hot, hot, yet cool and breezy
Caribbean women – we rule with an iron fist
We are lovers not fighters, although like a beast we can
We are carers, nurtures, and supporters
yes, we stand by our man
Caribbean women – we are highly intelligent
devoted to our families, full of spirituality
and can be overly religious
But don't let all of that fool you
because as good as we are with pen an paper
we can be just as skillful with a knife of a cutlass
Caribbean women – we are the real deal
what you see is what you get
for morals and values were instilled in us
from jump start, so if you are a gambler
on us you can bet.

Come Reason With Me

Come reason with me under the Baobab tree
About how change can't wait
but change must wait
for government is continuous
so, we know not who will determine our fate

Come reason with me under the Baobab tree
About the legalization and de-criminalization
of the sacramental herb
How rasta first discovered it
but all now can't recover it
since organize and centralize
to them is an unfamiliar verb

Come reason with me under the Baobab tree
About how parents today have dropped the ball
not teaching their children to know themselves at all
Then turn around and want to blame the youth
when they disconnect and embrace foreign concepts
as their truth

Come reason with me under the Baobab tree
About reparation and repatriation
about revolution and evolution
About the new world order versus the true world order
Come let's hold a vibe
reason with me under this Baobab tree.

Farewell My Daughter

(A tribute to Shermaine)

In my heart of hearts
beneath the sorrow, grief, and pain
I wear a permanent smile
at the mention of your name

You were chosen by God as my angel
to look over me from above
to comfort and protect me
and show me that I'll always be loved

I just can't hold back the tears
as I reflect on your forty eight years
You were my woman of business in every way
Gently guiding me with the choice words you say
Always re-assuring me, Mommy it will be ok

whenever I go off course and drift away
Although you've left this world
and now you've taken flight
I know that you are here with me in spirit
Each morning, noon, and night.

Queen Mother Roberts

Queen Mother Roberts
we are gathered here today
for we love, honor, respect and salute you
on this your very special day

Through all of your trials and tribulations
challenges, blood, sweat and tears
Our heavenly father has seen it fit
to bless you with an abundance of years

So, on your ninety ninth and moving forward
as you enjoy the gift of life each and every day
we pray that you will be covered by His blood
as you continue to let Jesus be your stay

Blessed 99th Earthday Queen Mother Roberts

Lady of Grace

(Molly's 60th Earthday)

A standing ovation is in order
as the room her presence fills
her energy, her disposition, her aura
captivates, mesmerizes, thrills
Yes, she is definitely an African queen
So, feast your eyes on royalty
Her Majesty, the lovely Queen Molly
An epitome of celestial beauty
Carolita, Alicia, Mols, call her what you will
her dimpled smile melts every heart
and commands all storms – peace be still
Girl, you are a modern-day Mother Teresa
so selfless, so giving, so true
so today we place 60 stars in your crown
as we celebrate, honor, and salute you.

Birth of An Angel

Why is it that some babies
enter this world and exit at the same time
Because some were destined for heaven
while others to earth were assigned
Not suggesting that it's not hard
for by no means is it an easy road
when for nine long months you have nurtured
and carried that special load

But God knows each and every one of us
before we were conceived in our mother's womb
He designed for us a divine purpose and plan
and is with us from the cradle to the tomb
So be strong my child and be of good cheer
for He will not give you more than you can bear

Don't you weep, don't you mourn, don't you cry
for your child is merely resting, she did not die
She earned her wings before touching this earth
So, blessed is your womb
for an angel you once birthed.

Get Ready and Stay Ready

As we gather here to bid our loved one adieu
we are reminded that this life is temporary
for we are only passing through
So, it matters not if you are rich or poor
illiterate or well learned
The fact is that from dust we came
and to dust we shall return
Earthly riches shall fade away
in the twinkling of an eye
but the blessings left for future generations
will live on long past the day we die
So now that you are blessed with the gift of life
find your purpose and pursue it with passion
Forget about confusion and strife
let serving God and others be your mission

Be kind, patient, considerate, loyal and true
longsuffering, loving, forgiving
putting God first in all that you do
For the day will come when it's your turn
in that casket to be present
Be sure with open arms the Lord will say
Well done, my good and faithful servant.

Just A Rose Will Do

Through the garden of life
take me for a ride
So that I may smell the flowers
while I am still alive

Show me how much you love me
show me how much you care
Show me that you are grateful
each and every day of the year

Don't wait until I lay in my coffin
to express your love through sorrow
For today is all that we have
we were never promised tomorrow

So now that I am here

please try your best to be sincere

For when my life on this earth is through

don't spend your money on wreaths

Just a rose will do.

We will be called oaks of righteousness......

Beauty for Ashes

Broken, discouraged and full of despair
trust in the Lord with all of thine heart
and have no fear
He promised to provide for all who grieve in Zion
the calm of a lamb and strength of a lion
instead of ashes
to bestow on them a crown of beauty
Ears shall truly hear and eyes shall see
for weeping endures only for a night
but at the dawning
there's oil of joy instead of mourning
Clothed in a garment of praise
and not one of despair
with a spirit of love and not a spirit of fear
We will be called oaks of righteousness
a planting of the Lord
Displaying His splendor as we pass the test
Standing on His promises
as He gives us beauty for ashes.

Smile For Life

Beauty is power and a smile is its sword
for as it cuts, it transforms your life
much like that of the umbilical chord
It is the key which unlocks many a frown
opens doors, closes arguments
lifts you up when you're feeling down
It is light in the window of your face
a vehicle on life's journey
which transports you to a higher place
Without apology, excuse or reason
a smile is always relevant, always in season
it is the sun which turns winter into summer
and makes a burden lighter
It costs nothing, but gives so much
And as such

I invite you to put on a smile each day
Before leaving home and being on your way
share it freely and in abundance
to your life it will add such substance
As you fight your battles
and trod through life mile by mile
Let there be peace on earth
and let it begin with a smile.

Four Hundred Years and Counting

It's been over four hundred years
since they've changed the name
but six and half a dozen is still the same
They no longer sell us but we've learned well
So, now our brothers and sisters for a joint we sell
Can you imagine the audacity
another sister born and raised in Africa
tries to disclaim my authenticity
Calling me a descendant of slaves
ss my ancestors roll in their graves
Remembering when
they were snatched from their father's hand
and transported from the mother land
Now the middle passage has been replaced
by the middle man who has no loyalty to
race

Once a hunted people like sheep and goats
we now simply cut each other's throats
Our race is being terrorized
we are under attack
It's because we've come a long way
why it's a long way back
But a journey of a thousand miles
begins with one step
So, let's organize and centralize my people
It's time to rep.

You Are an African Child

You are an African child
born happy and free
for your history does not begin with slavery
You were brought to Alliougana
in the womb of your ancestor
Who from massa's bitter cup did sip
bruised, battered, mind altered
by the sting of the whip
Robbed of your history
robbed of your mother's tongue
robbed of your culture
robbed of your ancestral knowledge
and wisdom
Yet unbroken in spirit
undefeated, your courage remained
for the blood of warriors and freedom fighters
run through your veins
So, you shall re-learn

Take the Sankofa journey back
to know thyself, you shall return
if not in body, in spirit and in mind
To embrace the beauty of your blackness
your authenticity, you are one of a kind
To re-claim your regal heritage
Prince and Princesses
Kings and Queens
sons and daughters of the Nile
For you are African, you are African
Yes, you are African my child.

The Confession

We came with our bibles and taught you to read
hands clasped, eyes closed, pay us no heed
while we demonized your spirituality
and robbed you of your traditions and culture
Blindfolded you with the image
of a blond-haired and blue-eyed Savior
Forget about giving praises to the Creator
to Ra for the gift of melanin
Replaced sUn with sOn to white wash your sin
Your holistic spiritual concepts
expressed through Ifa, Yoruba and Bantu
we feared, so called it witchcraft and voodoo
Paying homage and honoring your ancestors
we labelled worshipping the dead
although your blood-soaked tribal wear
was what we used to paint the sea red
The mighty healer who cleansed the leper
made the lame walk and the blind see

were quite often demonstrated
by your natural powers and ability
We taught you to love and respect your enemies
to not only trust but obey the slave master
Speak only when spoken to, shut your beak
Love those who hate you, turn the other cheek
To devalue your women, break the backs of your sons
with the rod of correction
But from Genesis, you have exodused
and now living in the days of Revelation
For with wisdom, you did not just get knowledge
but also innerstanding
veil removed to expose our heinous sin
Now the acid rain has gone and you can see
that what we did was rape you
of your authentic African spirituality
Now go worship your God
in the beauty of His holiness
For you were made in His image – Royal blessed.

Let it be God

By your fruits you shall be known
harvest manifested by the seeds you have sown
Be it of peace or that of discord
it's all documented in that final record
Whether you are planting in or out of season
whatever your motive, whatever your reason
Let it be God

Commit your works unto the Lord
make Him your habitation, your abode
For by Him your plans shall be established
while earthly kingdoms are being demolished
So, whatever your calling, whatever your story
give Him all honor, all praise and glory
Let it be God.

The dancing, the shouting the fasting for days
are of no effect if God is not truly being praised
For unlike man, God sees only the heart
and one day the good and the evil shall be set apart
So, let God be the source of your motivation
whatever the circumstances or the situation
Let it be God

Let it be God for He is the Alpha and Omega
Let it be God for He is our Lord and Savior
Let it be God for man is nothing but dust
Let it be God and in Him only put your trust.

Let it be God

Standing on the Promises of God

Lord, you promised
never to leave me nor forsake me
that I shall be rich and not beg bread
that the waters shall not overflow me
neither shall flames kindle upon my head
So, upon your word, upon this rock I stand
I'm standing on the promises of God

Lord, you promised
that if I honor my mother and my father
my days on this earth shall be long
I shall walk and not be weary
I shall run and not faint
in my weaknesses I shall be made strong
So, upon your word, upon this rock I stand
I'm standing on the promises of God

Lord, you promised
that weeping shall endure for a night
but joy, sweet joy comes in the morn
that you have gone to prepare a place for me
and one bright day you shall return
So, upon your word, upon this rock I stand
I'm standing on the promises of God

Lord, I am standing on your promises
for you shall not fail
I am standing on your promises
for you shall prevail
I am standing on your promises
for you are God and therefore cannot lie
So, I will be standing on your promises
until the day I die.

Standing on the promises of God

Practical Application

Teach the youth the truth

through practical application

From Genesis we have Exodused

we are now living in the days of Revelation

Teach the youth the truth

The challenge with today's youth

is that they demand the truth, the whole truth

and nothing but the truth

but parents are too busy

swimming in pools of hypocrisy

while our leaders are politricking

playing games of republican democracy

So, we the people must arise, open up our eyes

un-veil, un-mask, remove the disguise

which causes us only to shift the blame

but when the spit hits the fan

we hang our heads in shame

Our youth are being supervised and taught
By iPhone, YouTube and the tell-lie-vision
what's wrong from what's right
Some glued to the tube all day
from dawn to dusk, playing fort night
Yet we complain that they no longer play
marbles, spin tops, and such games
but who bought them the gadgets
which are destroying their brains
A people defeated, heads bowed in shame
realizing that parenting is serious business
It's definitely not a game
The "do as I say and not as I do" mentality
has cost us one too many a casualty
Lead by example, practice what you preach
unless the future generation
you are not trying to reach
For the youth of today, their name is Karma
They will grow up to bite you in the behind
Don't say I didn't warn ya.

A Wa Dem A Teach Dem

Teachers of today
are no longer tasked with the duty
of encouraging proper personal hygiene
manners, ethics, and morality
But somehow
they continue in these modern times
to teach our children nursery crimes
For crying out loud and for goodness sake
you know they still teaching the pickney them
about Christopher come buss us, Marco Polo
and Sir Frances Drake
instead of teaching them about our ancestors
local leaders, sons and daughters of the soil
Makeda, Nzingha and other Queens of the Nile

But I am calling on parents for the onus is on you
For you are your children's first teachers
that saying is absolutely true
Before you send them to church and school
first, teach them at home, don't raise no fool
Don't teach them *what*, but *how* to think
teach them to be conscious and mindful
from the fountain of wisdom to drink
Take my foolish advice
and teach your own pickney my friend
because inna disya time
Me no know 'wa dem a teach dem.

By What Measure

Plant seeds of knowledge

wisdom, understanding and truth

in the minds of our youth

for they must be consciously led

before they can consciously lead

It is they who will determine

the destiny of our nation

instruct them to build on a strong foundation

For wherever their hearts lie

therein will be their treasure

and by the measure they mete

they shall be measured

By what measure

do they determine their strength

Is it measured by height, breadth

width or length

By what measure

Do they determine their choices

Is it by technological devices

They must burn the tell-lie-vision

and use the mental capacity

of their infinite mind

as they embrace the value of their uniqueness

knowing that they are each one of a kind

Plant seeds of knowledge

wisdom, understanding and truth

in the minds of our youth.

Shattering Glass Ceilings

I AM SHATTERING GLASS CEILINGS

Shattering glass ceilings

on domestic violence and sexual abuse

Shattering glass ceilings

on human trafficking and drugs mis-use

Shattering glass ceilings

on LGBT rights and abortion

Shattering glass ceilings

on money laundering and extortion

I AM SHATTERING GLASS CEILINGS

Shattering glass ceilings

on false prophets as head of the church

Shattering glass ceilings

on it's a black life, so abandon the search

Shattering glass ceilings

on organs being harvested for sale

Shattering glass ceilings

on bbl's and trading melanin for pale

I AM SHATTERING GLASS CEILINGS

Shattering glass ceilings
on who's bringing guns into the country
Shattering glass ceilings
on child molestation and incest in the family
Shattering glass ceilings
on priests having nuns and doing our sons
Shattering glass ceilings
on the mis-leaders known as politicians

I AM SHATTERING GLASS CEILINGS

Shattering glass ceilings
on AIDS, cancer and Covid 19 vaccination
Shattering glass ceilings
on the real deal about marijuana legalization
Shattering glass ceilings
on stand your ground and police brutality
Shattering glass ceilings
on the anti-Christ and illuminati

I AM SHATTERING, SHATTERING SHATTERING GLASS CEILINGS.

I Am Sorry That You Are Sorry

As a people we have been programmed

to be too quick to say I'm sorry

Sorry to whom, for what, for being me

Honey child, there will be no apology

And furthermore

I am not sorry that the truth offends

I am not sorry that after you've been forgiven

there will be no amends

I am not sorry that I do not entertain hypocrisy

I am not sorry that from self-inflicted wounds

you bleed, and not me

I am not sorry that the tables have been turned

I am not sorry that it is now your turn

I am not sorry, so I decree and declare

burn Babylon burn

I am not sorry that karma is my friend and your enemy

I am not sorry that with 20/20 vision

you still refuse to see

but while you are at it

do not confuse sorry with empathy

For not only am I woke, conscious

empathetic and compassionate

I am also a torch bearer of my ancestors – lest I forget

I am sorry that you are sorry

But being sorry, just isn't me.

I Will Not Apologize

I will not apologize for embracing my culture and
acknowledging my history

I will not apologize for the spirit of my ancestor who
breathes and lives through me

I will not apologize for owning my blackness

my beauty, my boldness

for being an authentic and down to earth empress

I will not apologize for my bald head

after rocking dread locked hair

I will not apologize for always wearing

cultural attire with an African flair

I will not apologize nor will I withdraw

my request for reparations

I will not apologize for seeking true freedom long after
your declaration of emancipation

I will not apologize for refusing to wine, dine
and sip from your bitter colonial cup
I will not apologize for my absence at your hypocrites
conventions, and that's what's up
I will not apologize even when my neck
is under your knee
I will not apologize for there is absolutely
no need for an apology

I will not apologize.

A father should not only be fruitful

But a God-fearing man......

Blessed Father's Day

A father should not only be fruitful
but a God-fearing man
who leads his wife and children
according to God's plan

He is blessed with strength and valor
wisdom, knowledge, and understanding
he supports, provides, and protects
although life at times can be demanding

He is the first role model for his children
he teaches them right from wrong
he raises them with Godly principles
for even in his weakness, he is made strong

So, I am calling on all of the fathers
to be good parents, it matters not the amount
for God has assigned you this role
and one day, you will have to give an account.

Hey Mr Saxophone man

Blowing me softly with his sax.......

The Sax Man

Under star-lit skies, dining on the beach
Pink sand kissed by turquoise seas all within reach
Trying to resist temptation as best as I can
but I'm just blown away by the Saxophone Man
The food is delish, cocktails right
ambience set, the mood is just tight
Trying to resist temptation as best as I can
but I'm simply blown away by the Saxophone Man
The way he wraps his lips around that joint
eyes so compelling, ah yes, I get the point
Still trying to resist temptation as best as I can
but I'm just blown away by the Saxophone
What the heck, life is for living
enjoy it while you can
tonight, tonight, tonight
I'm gonna get me some of that Saxophone Man.

Montserrat Strong

Can you believe it's been thirty years
since life as we knew it?
It was 1995 when the volcano erupted
Yes, she finally blew it
Reading us what was apparently our last rights
talking about ashes to ashes
but had to cease and settle
when it came down to dust to dust
for the fiery grave could not hold us down
resurrection was a must
For we are a people resilient
long-suffering courageous and strong
Although we may be short in numbers
we stand tall for the land to which we belong
Montserrat, oh Montserrat
Emerald Isle of the Caribbean Sea
No matter where our seeds may be scattered
we stay loyal to thee

We will keep our vibrant culture alive
while embracing our new truths
instilling traditional values in our younger generation
from the days of their youth
Teaching them not only about Masquerades
John Bull and Miss Goosey
but about Cudjoe, W.H. Bramble and John Bassey
About Sir Howard Fergus, David Edgecombe
Jim Allen, and oh, you thought that I forgot
our very own, the Mighty Arrow
who long before global warming
had the entire world feeling hot, hot, hot
Of the healing benefits of herbs
How to make cassava bread and ducna
Plate tart, sugar cake, guava cheese
ginger stick, and our infamous goat water
And I can go on and on, but time does not permit
So, from Long Ground to Plymouth
St. Patrick's to St. Johns
We say thanks to all who over the years
held our hand and helped us to remain strong
Thirty years and counting strong – Montserrat strong.

Back to Montserrat Sistah Flarry

Back to Montserrat, Sistah Flarry
you no know wa you da say
you forgat a de volcano erupt
and cause so good all awee fu run go a de UK
Oooh, you tyud o' de cold weather
de dampness a get to you bone
So you rather go home whey you can chillax
and sun you kin pan toan
Well, according to Dr. Ryan
and the scientists at the MVO
although she may seem dormant for a while
if you tek a closer look
de volcano still a bubble and bwile
But me undustan
you tired o' de hustle and bustle
Tired fe run ketch train and bus
and de likkle pittance you a get a mont time
it no really wot de fuss

while all kinda foreigner inna Montserrat
a help fe rebuild yes, but a live larger than life
Gway wid you tantiborginess and tap hold strife
But you can't even afford fe buy wan ticket
fu come home fu Christmus
You inna Inglun a ketch hell
So, in all honesty, me can't say me blame you
all me coulda say, a walk good gyel
Beeause fan de time you reach Antigua
and drive to de Montserrat ferry
wey look lek one cruise ship
you done feel de weight lif arf you back
although you no reach de end o' you trip
and when you kiss de grung inna Montserrat
and bless you yeye pan de new development
dung a Likkle Bay
you wonda why you tek um pan yourself
inna de fuss place, fe jump ship and go a de UK
But swallow you pride gyel
just come, a Montserrat you barn
and a Montserrat you rear
Nobody can run you fram whey you come fram
So you can go and come as you like and have no fear.

Taste Of The Caribbean

One of the things on my bucket list
was to travel each Caribbean island
and sample their national dish

My first stop was Anguilla
for some pigeon peas and rice
ahyou look a hell, what a thing taste nice

Next, I went over to Antigua/Barbuda
for steam fish, fungi, and pepper pot
like Burning Flames, that ish was hot, hot, hot

Talking about hot, hot, hot
you know I had to go home to Montserrat
Gyel, Montserratian mek de best goat water
You haffe come and check us out
we put the pestle to the mortar

Well, you know that from Montserrat
Guadeloupe is right next door
So, I had to hop, skip and jump over
for some pork colombo for sure

Then it was over to sugar city St. Kitts/Nevis
for some saltfish, plantain,
and oh so delicious coconut dumplin
When I tell you one pound of sugar
ain't enough pound of sugar
for a thorough oil dung
I had to head to the spice isle of Grenada

Then it was time to link up
with my good friend Asa Banton
in Dominica for Creole Fest
for when it comes to Callaloo
Hands down, they have the very best

Now on to St. Lucia
For some saltfish and green fig
Sakafet
that thing had me doing the "food taste good" jig

Now you know I had to go
to St. Vincent and the Grenadines
For what was my favorite dish
Roast breadfruit, fried Jacks and black fish

Barbados, Barbados, Barbados
I just had to close my eyes and make a wish
for their mouth-watering cou-cou and flying fish

And you know that she is Trini to the bone for true
the way she whips up that pelau and callaloo

Well, for a much-needed break
I took a weekend cruise to the Bahamas
for some conch salad, conch chowder
and finger licking conch fritters

And although ackee and salt fish
is their national dish
I must admit that the Jamaican man
definitely have the best jerk hand

Now, what can I say but Sak-pase'
You actually thought I left out Haiti
There's no way
Before I wrapped up this Caribbean food tasting tour
I had to get me some griot for sure.

SECTION 2
SHORT STORIES

Montserrat has the sweetest mangoes
say me tell you so
Whether St Lucian, turpentine, grafted
julie, hairy, or peter kidney
Just set up a bucket of water under a shady tree
without making any fuss, we just pound story
and eat 'till we belly buss'.

How Sissy Donkey Lost Her Tail

Once upon a time, not so long ago, on the enchanted island of Montserrat in the picturesque village of Harris' lived a happy donkey family. Ma and Pa donkey, and their two children Bo and Sissy.

Sissy was the baby but she was growing up real fast and it was going to be soon time for her to graze on her own. It was decided that her brother Bo should take her from Muss Ghaut to Paradise to teach her what she should and should not eat.

So, one bright and sunny Monday morning, they started off on their *"you are what you eat"* expedition.

They took a short cut below the market, passed brother John and Marse Willie White's houses to end up by the big school, before crossing Maggie Ghaut to get to Paradise.

Well, from the time they hit Sunter Street, they started to smell the fresh fruits, herbs and vegetables from Shan's garden. Thankfully, Shan was not at home, he was most likely at Parson Greer's Rum Shop having breakfast. Well, Bo and Sissy decided to have breakfast also. They ate some potato vines, cabbage, carrots, tomatoes, and oh so delicious mangoes that fell under the tree.

After they had their fill, they decided to cross the street to be on the side of Paradise. On their way down the narrow winding path to Maggie Ghaut, Bo pointed out a wild tamarind tree and told Sissy that by no means should she eat from that tree. Sissy could not understand why, and Bo chose not to tell her. He just repeated what Ma Donkey would say, "because I say so," they reached Maggie Ghaut, drank some sweet running water, and crossed over to Paradise.

Even the air felt different over in Paradise. The skies looked bluer, the breeze felt cooler, the grass was greener, it truly lived up to it's name.

They passed a few people on their way. Nickey Weeks had a crocus bag of potatoes on his head, and the boys Ashley and Len for Leah Greer were going to cork a coal pit which caught a draft. This, they observed from their house on Harris' Hill.

Bo and Sissy rested for a while under a loblolly tree where they chewed on some sticky black fruit which tasted like licorice. There were fields of guava, guava plum, blueberries and blackberries. Cows were grazing and bees were buzzing. They felt as though they died and went to heaven.

They were actually there for quite a few hours because the shadows of the evening were creeping in, so they realized that it was time to head back home. On their way back, Bo saw his girlfriend Girlie Donkey grazing not too far off, and went over to speak to her, leaving Sissy right next to a wild tamarind tree. Sissy decided to eat from the forbidden tree and quickly wipe her mouth before Bo returned. They got back home just before sun set and turned in for the night.

A few days later, Ma Donkey noticed that Sissy was shedding her tail and scolded Bo, asking "why did you let her eat from a wild tamarind tree?" Bo explained to his mom that he specifically told Sissy not to eat from the wild tamarind tree, and so she did not. Little did he know what transpired when he went to talk to Girlie. But Ma was convinced that she had to eat from that tree which caused the hair on her tail to be falling off, so Ma called Sissy and demanded that she told the truth about eating from the wild tamarind tree. Sissy could not understand how they knew that she ate from that tree. Ma Donkey explained to her the importance of obedience, because *"what sweet in donkey mouth can be bitter in her tail."*

Hold Him Joe

Talking about donkey stories, Marse Joe had a donkey named Peetah. Peetah was a loyal and reliable companion. Every day they had the same routine. After breakfast, Marse Joe would get a bucket of mangoes, a bucket of water, and go under a coconut tree in the yard. Peetah was tied to a guinep tree, with enough rope to reach Marse Joe under the coconut tree.

Marse Joe would polish (eat) all of the mangoes, while Peetah eat the skins and seeds. He would have several conversations throughout the day with Peetah because he would say that man to man is so unjust, he didn't know who the hell to trust.

One could hear his wife cursing at him throughout the day, complaining that he shows the darn donkey more affection than her. Around two o'clock she would put on a pot of rice, chicken back and neck and some boiled sweet potatoes and green bananas. Every other day or so, she would put a slice of roast breadfruit on the side. Marse Joe would have his fill, while Peetah was treated to the sweet potato, green banana and breadfruit peels.

Around four o'clock was time for them to hit the road. Parson Greer Rum Shop – here they come. Marse Joe would sit upright, proud as a peacock on Peetah's back as he was transported to his usual destination of choice. There he would plaster (drink) rum, brandy, vodka, whatever was available with his friends and fellow villagers.

When it was time to go home, he would be so drunk, that someone would have to throw him over Peektah's back like a sack of potatoes and Peetah would take him straight home. When they got home, Peetah would stoop to the ground so he could gently slide off, and as the saying goes, "*way e drap e tap*" because that's where he would sleep for most of the night until he is woken by the sound of his wife complaining about him and his Jackass.

Give The Child My Name

Growing up as a child, my mother told us the story about our brother Ezra and how he got the pet name "Jackie." As I grew older, I realized that he was not the only one, even our famous cricketer Jim Allen shared the same experience. So how did they get these names?

Well, the story is told that whenever an elder die and want to live on, they come back from the grave and claim a child to be called by their name. If the child is not given that name at birth, the child would be sick until he/she is given the name. They would sometimes appear in a dream, advising the parent to give the child their name, or they would have the child display some of their characteristics which will point out to the parents who the child remind them of.

So, in my brother Ezra's case, he was very sick as a child and no matter what my mother tried, nothing seemed to work. One night, Bo Jackie, an elder from the village who passed on earlier appeared to her in a dream. She said that she was walking along a narrow path when she came upon Bo Jackie. She said, *"Good night Bo Jackie,"* but he shrugged his shoulders and said, *"Don't tell me howdy, because you have the little boy over there and you wouldn't give him my name."* The next morning when Ezra woke up and my mom called him, he said, *"don't call me Ezra, my name is Jackie."* From that day forward he was not sick anymore and everyone called him Jackie

Back To The Dust

Sundays in Montserrat were synonymous with church – a hearty saltfish breakfast in the morning, followed by morning service, a nice lunch, followed by visiting shut-in friends and relatives or Sunday school, and back to evening service.

One evening service that stands out in my mind throughout the years, was one held at the Church of God of Prophecy in Harris' which was run by Brother Rainey and Sister Katie. It was a small wooden structure, possibly 12 x 14, but appeared much bigger at the time. The floor and wooden pews would creak as members trickled in adorned in their stiffly starched and mothball-scented Sunday best.

This particular night was crusade night. Lord have mercy, the sound of the electric guitar was as if the trumpets were sounding on judgement day. Sister Violet was doing the holy ghost dance, while brother Melroy was talking in tongues. Brother Jerry did not make it any easier, the way he was beating those drums – the cymbals made my poor little heart race faster. Lord, what did I get myself into. Just to get a little piece of guava cheese and extra strong candy from Ma wasn't worth this torture. But be as it may, I was already in it to win it. The fright made me want to pee, but little girls were not allowed to go to the outside church latrine at night, so I had to hold my peace.

The collection plate was passed around, and I put in the two ten cent and kept back the five cents to buy sweets the next day on my way to school. Now I look back and wonder if God would punish me for stealing from him by not putting in all the money that I was given for collection back then.

Anyhow, it was time for the Word. Brother Rainey gave brief opening remarks, followed by a movie called "*The Burning Hell.*" When I tell you scary movie, I mean scary movie. Beetlejuice, The Exorcist and Freddie Crouger can't hold a candle to it. It was basically encouraging you to give your life to Christ, because if you are not saved, when you die, you will go to hell. It shared what hell would be like. To rub it in, at the end of the movie, they had altar call while singing the song "*Back to the dust.*"

Back to the dust, back to the dust, back to the dust we must go... The entire congregation went up to the altar to get saved. Even some people who were already saved, went up just to be double sure. The entire village accepted Jesus Christ as their Lord and Savior, because after going back to the dust, they did not want to experience the *burning hell*.

Rum 'Till I Die

Long before Adesh Samaroo of Trinidad sang the calypso *"Rum 'till I die, she told me she don't love me and that's the reason why...,"* we had our own *"Rum 'Till I die"* tales in my little country. This, however, was not a love story. It was a *Pay me what you owe me or else* story.

School children said that my uncle Shan, a man named Nickie Weeks and a man named Coolumarlo, among others, went to a watery grave filled with spirits due to bad credit, if you know what I mean.

They would hang out by a rum shop in the village every day and do what rum men (alcoholics) do. They would drink to their heart's content and their livers dis-content. They would *ole talk*, reason without a sense of reason, and occasionally get in a brawl. The rum shop was a community gathering place which was like a watering hole for two-legged animals.

Well as the story goes, the proprietor of the rum shop made a confession on his dying bed about the number of people who he poisoned in rum because they owed him. The aforementioned were only a few names that he was able to spew out before they stuffed his mouth with cloth so that he could not name any other names. I guess it was a case of mouth open and story jump out or better yet mouth stuff after he said more than enough. I guess they did not drink sweet sugar water or turpentine before they went out drinking, so it was *Rum 'Till They Die*.

The Cesspool Rules

There were several rivers and water holes in Harris' village. One notorious hole was the Cesspool. At the mention of this name, one automatically thinks sewage, or something that stinks. Well, I will let you be the Judge.

My ninety one year old cousin was sharing *ole time* stories with me, when he stumbled across the Cesspool. So, apparently, when Bobo Bramble (a well-known obeah man in the village) finish taking demonic spirits out of people by giving them a bush bath, he would pour the demon infused water in a can, put the lid on, and someone would have to walk down to Cesspool, turn their back, throw the sealed can over their shoulder into the water hole and not look back. Usually, a cat who stays in the area would start following them and meowing, but they were not supposed to look back at the cat either. Once the can was thrown in the hole, the possessed individual would be free of the spirit and be healed.

So, one day, Bobo Bramble took a demon out of a young boy and his father was tasked with the responsibility of going to the Cesspool to dispose of the spirit. He was given the specific instructions as stated above. But I guess he either didn't, believe in the nonsense, or was just hardheaded, so mister man decided to open the pan, throw out the water in the pool, and take the empty pan back home. Guess he couldn't spare the pan. Well, the moment he did that, the boy died in the house. When he got back home, with the empty pan, they realized what happened. He cost his son's life by not following instructions. From that day forward, his wife never spoke to him again until the day he died.

No Nose Leah

Leah was a beautiful child, who out of jealousy they spoiled her nose, and although many pretend not to, they very well know how the story goes.

She said that her mother never really loved her because she claimed that she was the product of rape. Her father travelled to the United States of America and settled in the Boston, Massachusetts area, where he became a very successful realtor. As a young girl, Leah took care of her father's mother – her grandmother Grand Mattie. Grand Mattie was bedridden and depended on Leah as her caregiver. When she prepared meals for Grand Mattie, some of her cousins would come around and eat some of her tasty dishes off Grand Mattie's plate, and she would chase them away, so that Grand Mattie would eat enough to stay strong. Grand Mattie eventually passed, but lived a long and happy life, thanks to the care that she got from Leah.

Leah's father heard about the excellent care that his daughter was giving to his mother, and he was well pleased. As he got down in age, he became ill and asked Leah to travel to America to care for him. However, his wife, from whom he was separated due to incest on her part decided that Leah, who was a bastard child, would not gain more than her lawful children, so she set out to make sure that the trip to America never happened. She went to an obeah woman, got some powder, and sprinkled it on Leah's pillow. After inhaling it while she slept, Leah woke up with pimples on her nose and a terrible headache. As time passed, the pimples turned into sores that would not heal, and the headaches intensified. One day, someone came to her house and told her mother that she should take her to get looked after, because her illness was not normal. After doing so, Leah was healed but the damage was already done. Her nose was deformed. Her father eventually died and left a hefty inheritance for Leah. One of her sisters in America sent papers for her to sign making her the Administrator of their father's estate. By signing those papers, Leah signed away her inheritance.

Although they spoiled her nose and robbed her of her inheritance, Leah went on to have a good life because her sense of humor, words of wisdom, beautiful, warm, and loving personality was magnetic. She gave birth to one of the most beautiful girls in Montserrat and lived until she was 96 years old. Leah was my mother.

How The Fairy Healed My Crappax

Now this is what you call a true fairy tale.

once upon a time, on the enchanted island of Montserrat fairies we spotted like shooting stars. We knew that they were female based on their long flowing hair, and breasts long down to their waist.

The fairies were like spirits who would correct rude children. If you disobeyed your parents, the fairies would give you a good spanking.

Sambo was one of the boys in the village who was plagued by the condition called crappax. Crappax was when the heel was dry and cracked with deep crevices. One's heel could not touch the ground when they had crappax, because it was very painful. They had to walk on their toes. Deep inside the crevice is what they called the gut, and the only way to get the gut out so that one could be healed, was to rub the crevices with a soft stone called lyme until the gut came out. This was not an easy task.

So, one day, Sambo was walking on his toes along this short cut through Cocoa Alley when he spotted a fairy. One look at the long breasts and he took off running. Sambo was never so scared in his life. He ran and ran, trying to outrun this fairy but he did not even realize that his heels were touching the ground. When the fairy was no longer in sight, Sambo looked down on his bloody heel and realized that it was touching the ground and the painful crappax was gone. He started to sing, "O lam O lam, whey me crappax gone?"

And that's how his crappax was healed. So, the next time you come in contact with a fairy and you have an existing condition, like Sambo, perhaps you can run it off.

Penny Fart

I have heard the saying "a penny for your thoughts." But I must admit that until now, I've never heard of penny fart.

Growing up in Montserrat, one can acquire a nickname that can stick for the rest of your life based on many things. The way you look, the way you walk, the way you talk, an incident, your grandparents' name, etc.

So how did Phillip and his son Matthew get their nickname?

Well as the story goes, Phillip worked at Farms Estate for a man named Karl Hollinder. Mr. Hollinder was a prankster who would engage his workers from time to time in games and challenges, to keep their spirits up.

One day, Mr. Hollinder decided to have a fart competition. The person who could pass the loudest fart would win a cash prize.

Well, Phillip was known for his notorious farts, so he was sure that he could easily win this competition. However, Lady Luck was not on his side that day. Chest out, he walked to the middle of the circle of men, took a deep breath, and pressed down to let out what was supposed to be a thunderous fart, but all that managed to come out was a little squeak. They all laughed at him. This was disappointing. That day, he rated very low on the fart scale, so Mr Hollinder declared that it was only worth a penny.

From that day, he earned the name Penny Fart. Later on in life as he grew up and had children, his son Matthew inherited the name of his father Penny Fart because he was very angry when they called him that name, so it made the name stick even more.

I think I would rather get a penny for my thoughts than a penny for my fart.

Nick Names

Talking about nick names, Montserratians were famous for labeling you. Here are some of the nicknames I remember growing up in Harris village:

You already know how Phillip came by *Penny Fart*
But that's only where the nickname story start.
A man named Daniel who lived with Miss Winny
Was called *Scarce o' Fat* because he was so skinny.

There was this guy who made all animals his pet
He had sex with them, so they called him *the vet*.
Then we use to ride Errol, boy could he run fast
That's how he got the notorious name *Bo Harse*.

When Jim Allen signed up for World Series Cricket
We called him *Kerry Packer-* he did hold his wicket.
The little underwear thief was skillful you see
That's how he got the name *BeeBee Panty*.

A girl with real skinny legs, we called *Bagga Foot*

And my cousin from on the hill, we called him Tuut.

Poor Cheedo was so sweet when begging for money

that they couldn't help but call him *Parpa Honey*

Prison couldn't hold them if nicknaming was a crime

For since I've known myself, it was like learning nursey rhyme.

SECTION 3

HEAL THYSELF

Body, Mind & Spirit

Mother Earth Beckons

Mother Earth beckons

Your health is your wealth

Return to nature and heal thyself

Behold, Jah has given I and I every herb yielding seed

Every green herb for food

Their leaves will not whither, and their fruit will not fail and the leaves of the tree

Are for the healing of the nation

And so it is!

Natural Livity

Trodding Rastafari taught me a natural livity
to embrace nature, honor all that lives
to express my creativity.

The use of herbs for medicine and tradition
to value space, to value time
to be about my divinely purposed mission.

Trodding Rastafari taught me to be a naturalist
to burn fire on Babylonian system
while standing firm and ruling with an iron fist.

Trodding Rastafari taught me to walk in love and unity
to heal myself of all dis-eases
To rise to the righteousness and trod holy.

Healing of the Nation

Not only is this our holy sacrament

It is the healing of the nation
the cure for cancers and other diseases
To pass from generation to generation.

Nature's Medicine Chest

Purslane

Vervaine

Moringa

Mimosa

Chick weed

Anise seed

Without disregarding the rest

the above are some must haves'

in your Mother Nature's Medicine Chest.

GLOSSARY

Here you will find the definition of words and phrases unique to this book's setting to aid with reader comprehension.

Alliouagana	The original name of the island of Montserrat by the early inhabitants (the Tainos), meaning land of Prickly Bush.
Arf	Off
Ayou look a hell	Anguillan slang
Ayou oh	Montserratian slang
A wa dem a teach dem	What are they teaching them
Awee	Us
Bongo Natty	Naturally matted hair
Buss	Burst
Bwile	Boil
Crappax	Disease
Dem	Them
Disya	This
Drap	Drop
E	It
Fugat	Forgot
Gyel	Girl
Hog wash	Nonsense
Inglun	England
Ital	Natural plant-based diet

Kin	Skin
Likkle	Little
Livity	Lifestyle
Me no Know	I don't know
Mek	Make
Nyabinghi	Spiritual tradition / Branch of Rastafari
Pickney	Child
Sakafet	St. Lucian slang
Sak-pase	Haitian slang
Tantiborginess	Confusion
Tap	Stop
Tayud	Tired
Tek	Take
Tell-lie-vision	Television
'til	Until
Toan	Stone
Trodding	Walking
Undustan	Understand
Wa	What
Whey	Where
Wot	Worth
Ya	Here

The End of the Beginning

*The Yabba Pot is now bubbling
I have definitely stirred it up
I'm drinking from my saucer
For overflowing is my cup.*

*Maureen "Greer" Lee
"The Sankofa Lady"*

www.ingramcontent.com/pod-product-compliance
Lightning Source LLC
LaVergne TN
LVHW021356080426
835508LV00020B/2298